Welcome to Princesses and Their Dragons Coloring Book

By: AH64Designs

Inside you will find 20 full pages of adorable fantasy inspired Princesses and Dragons coloring art.

Never stop having fun!

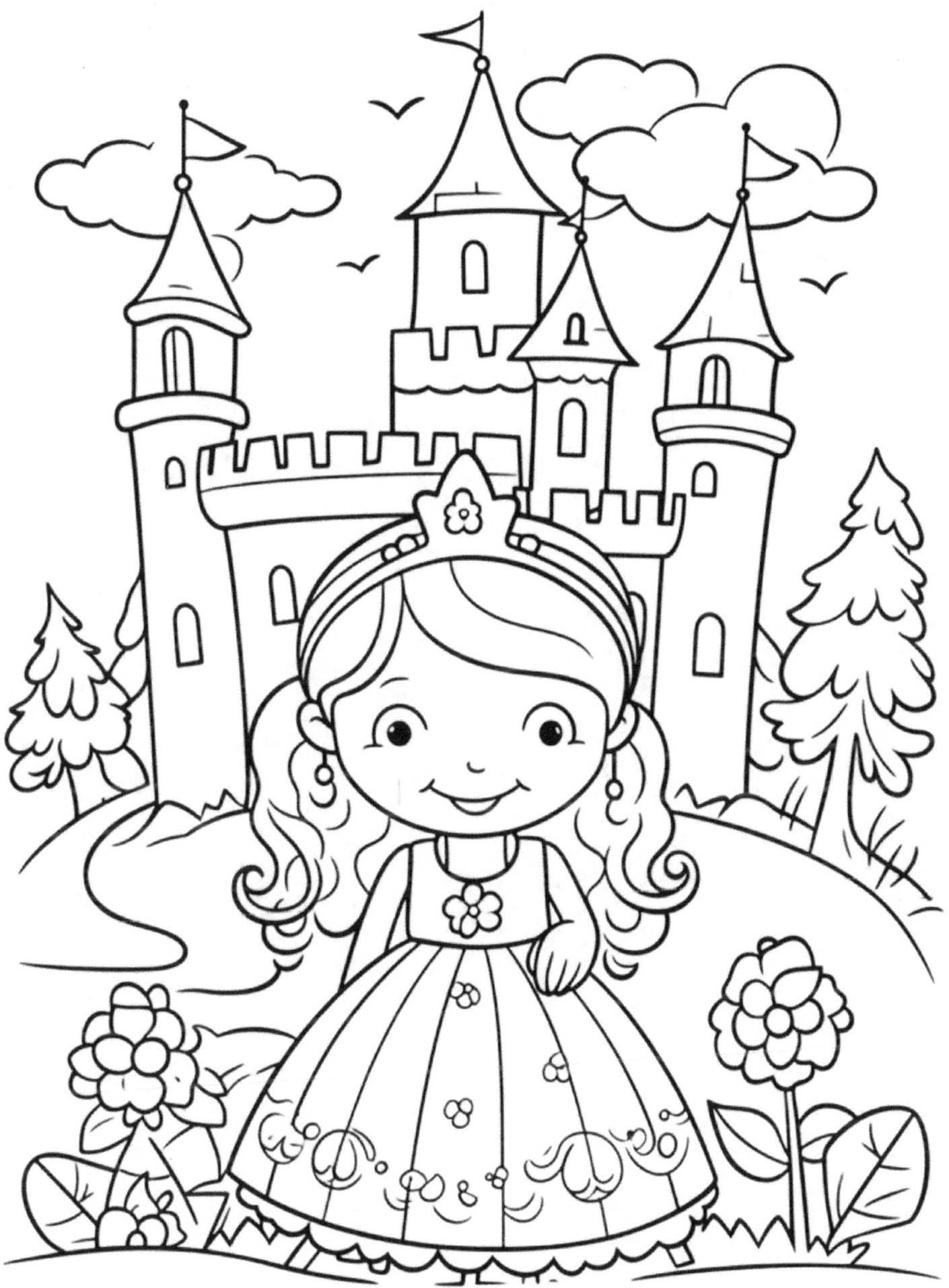

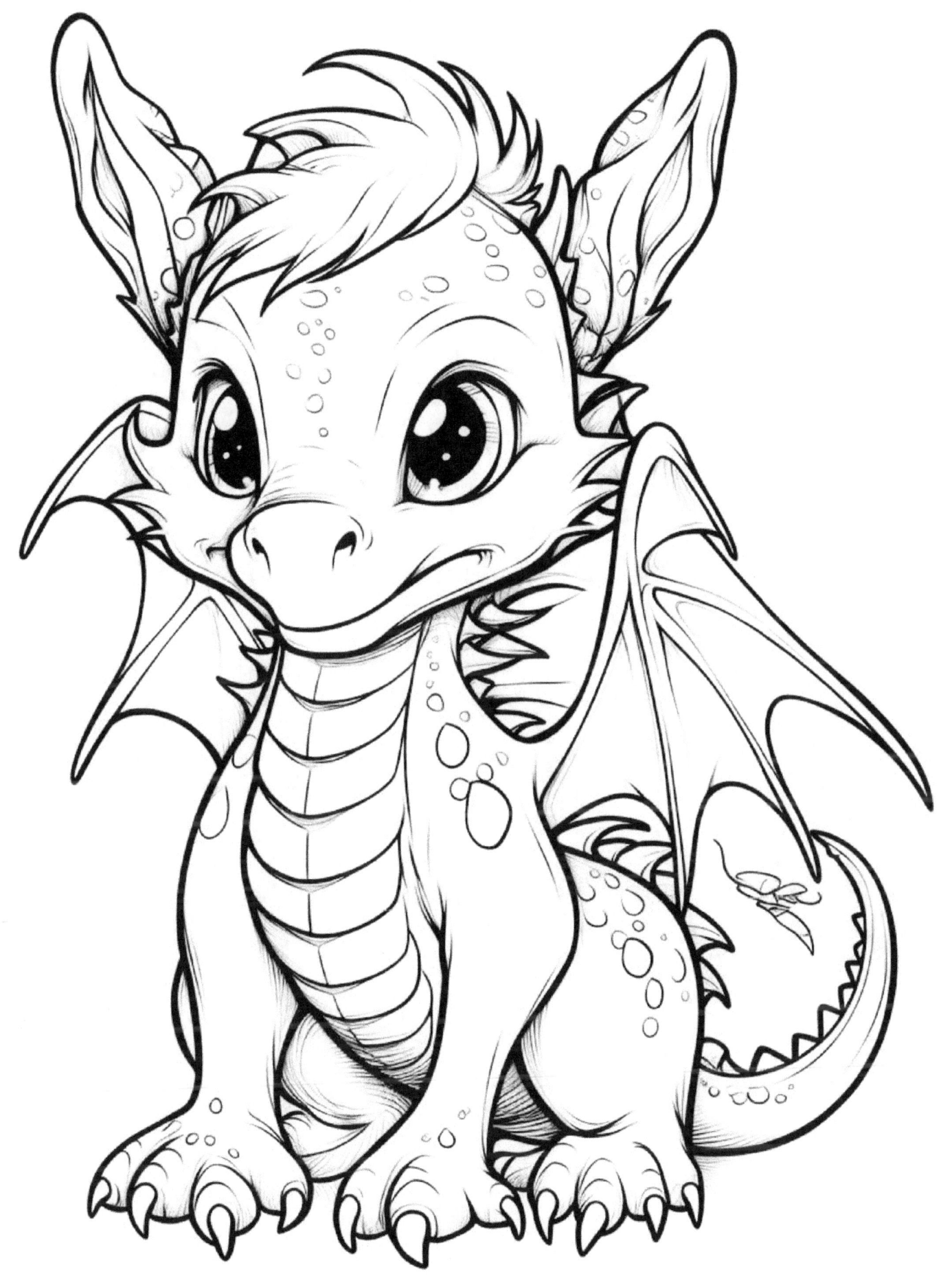

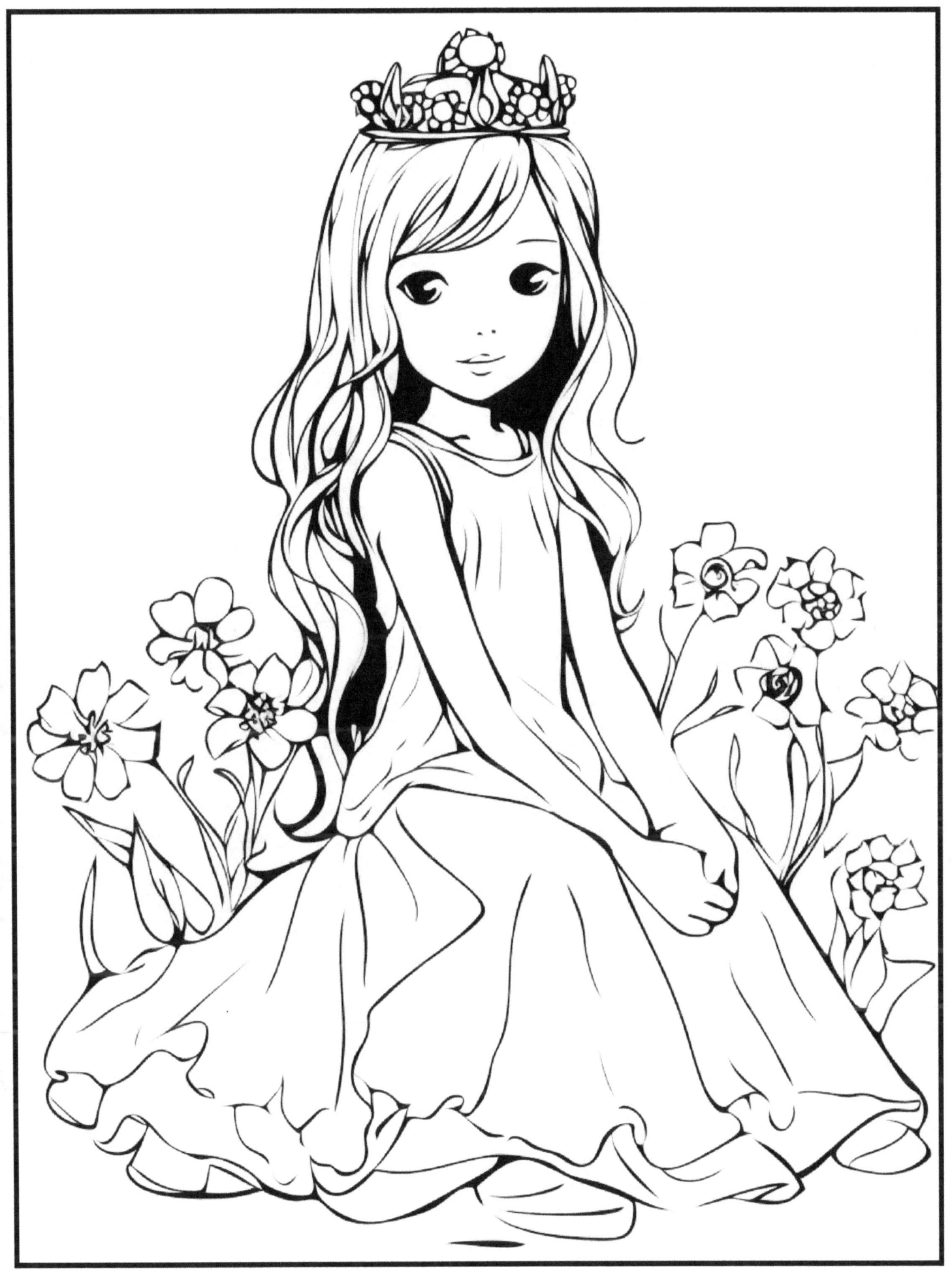

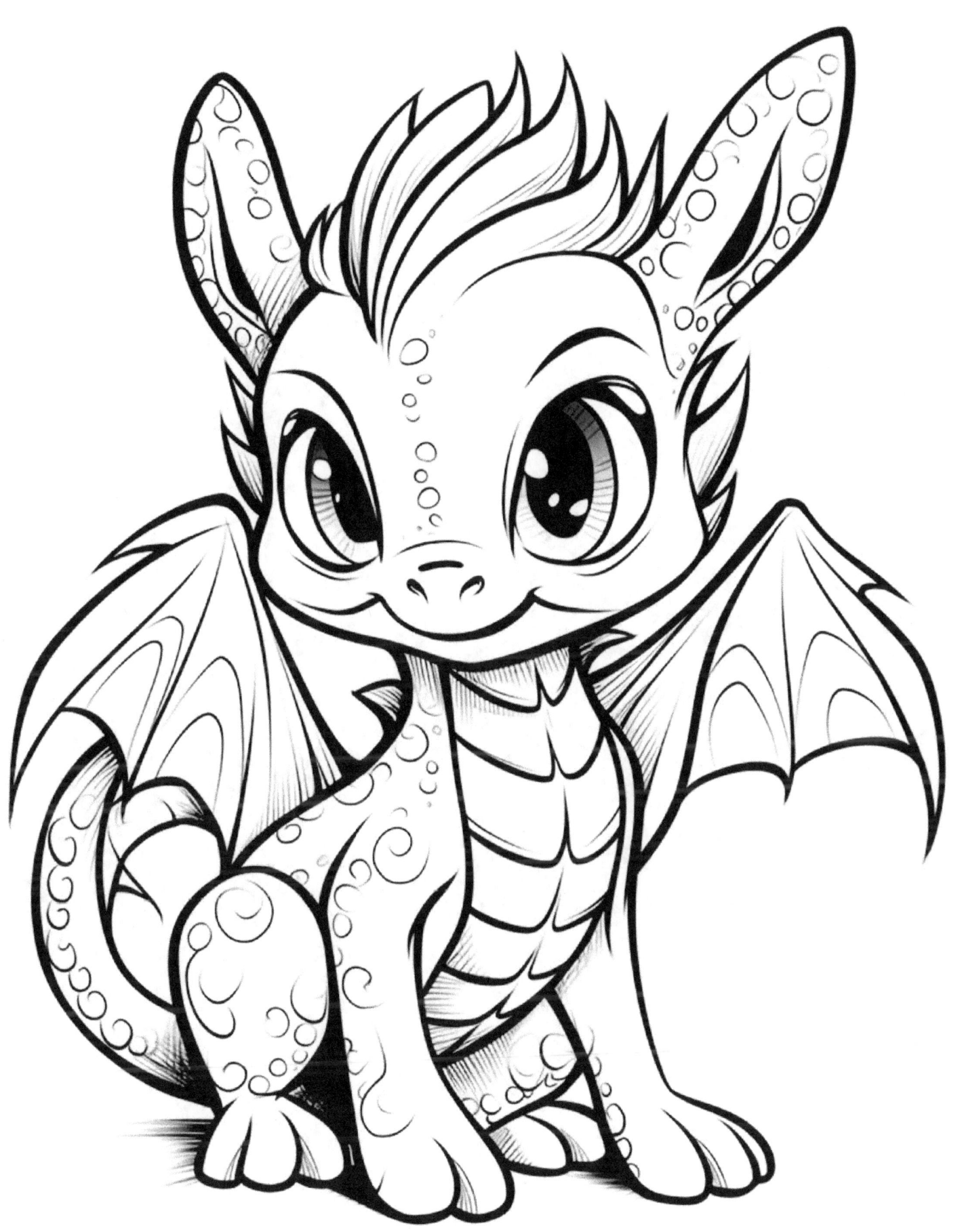

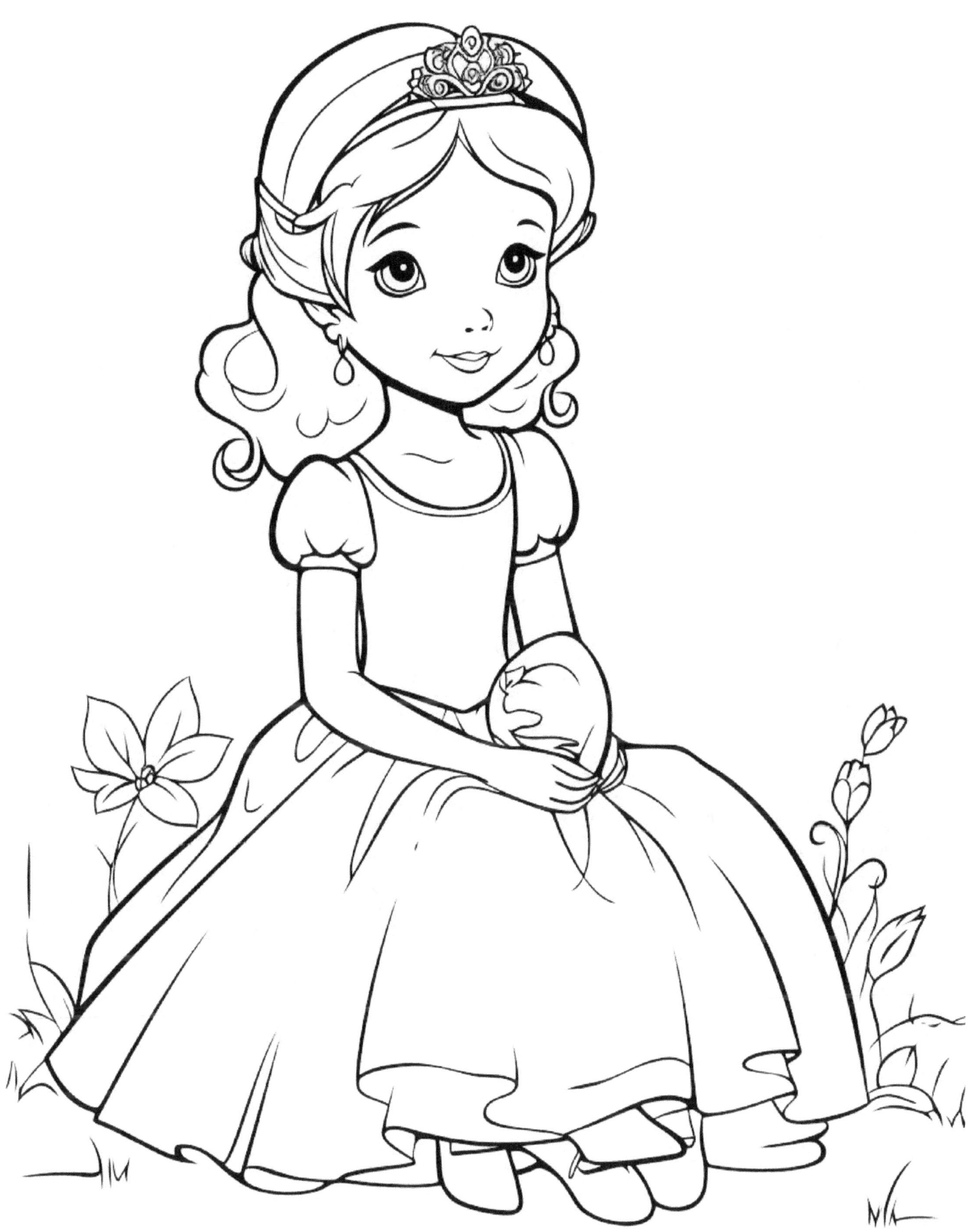

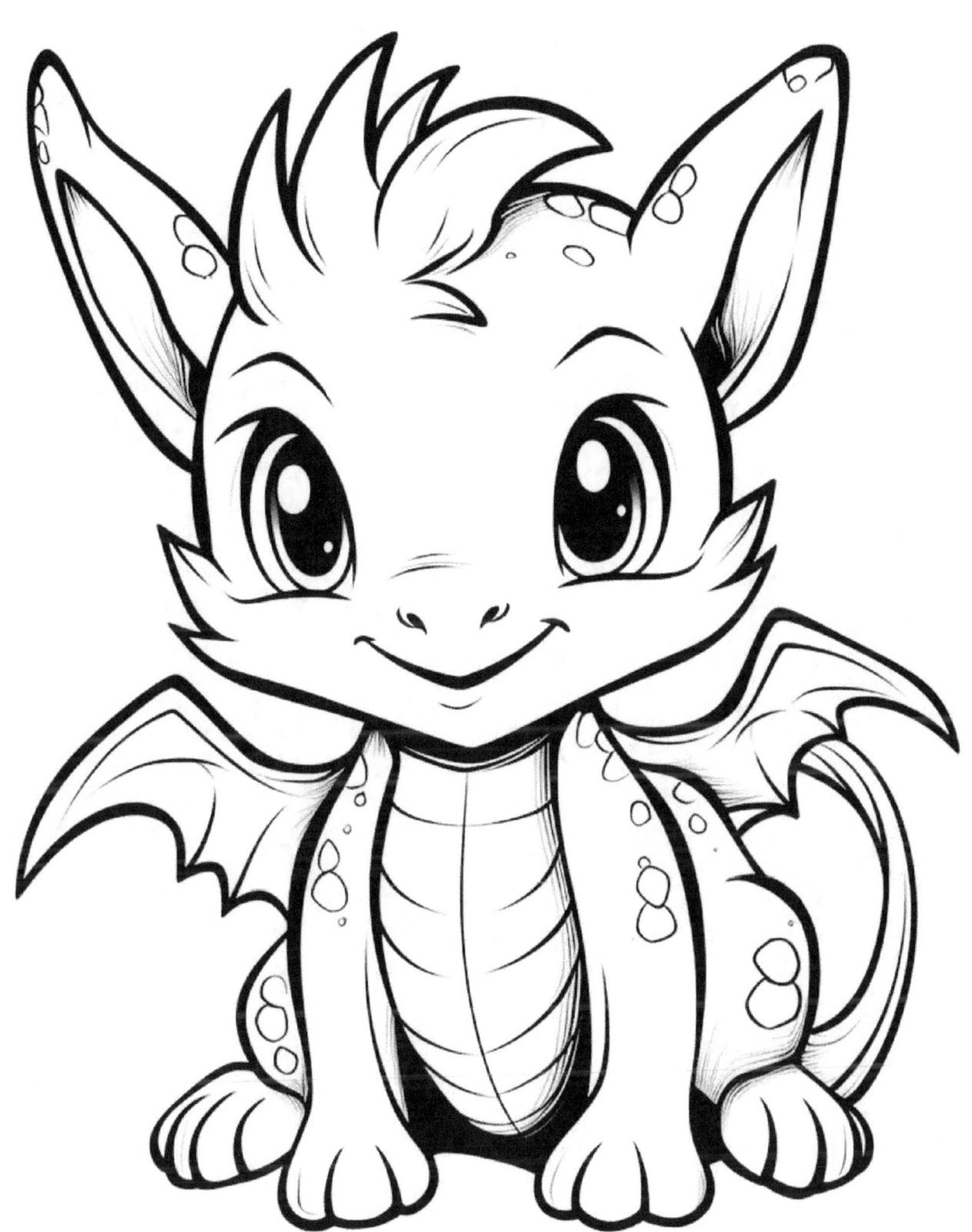

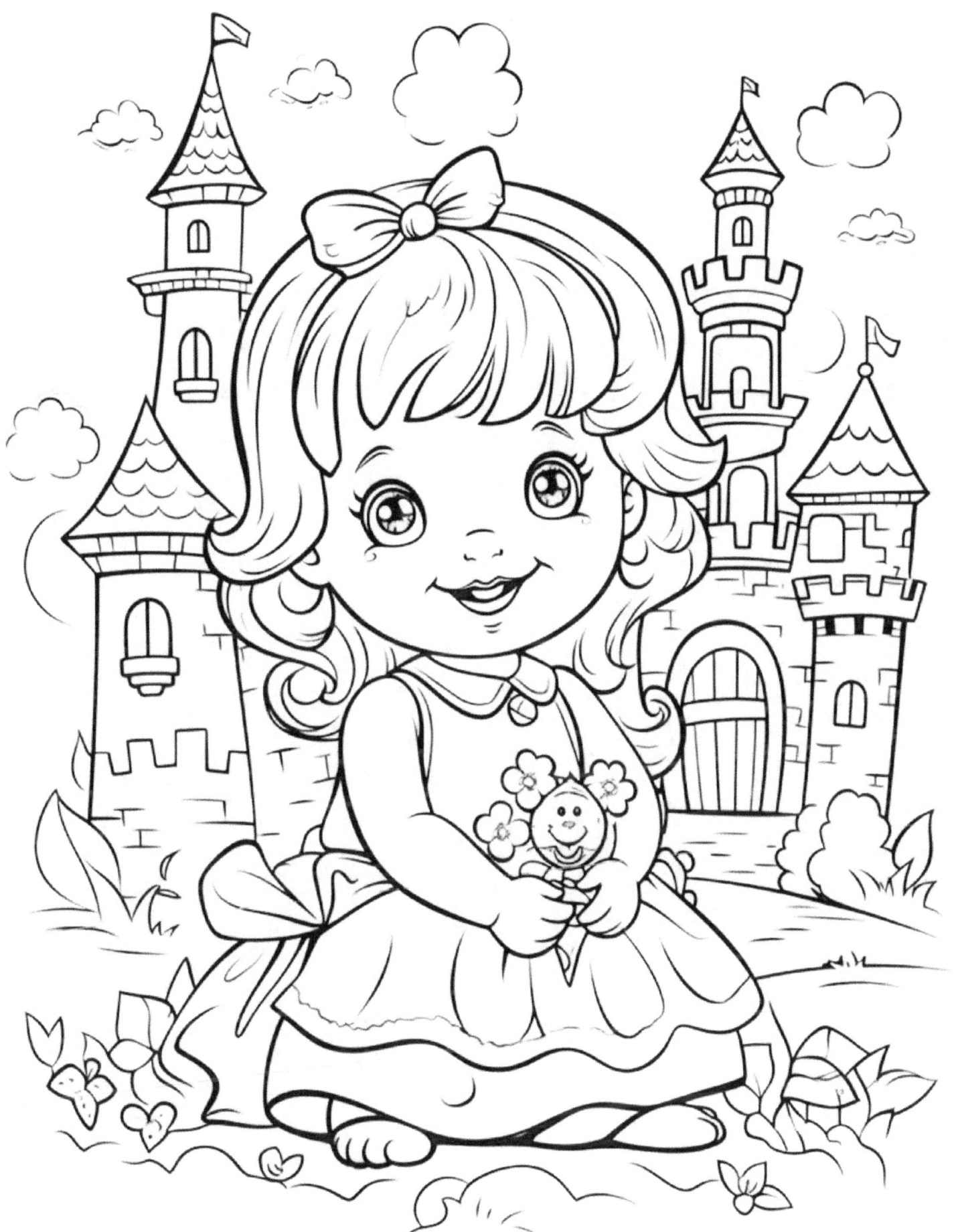

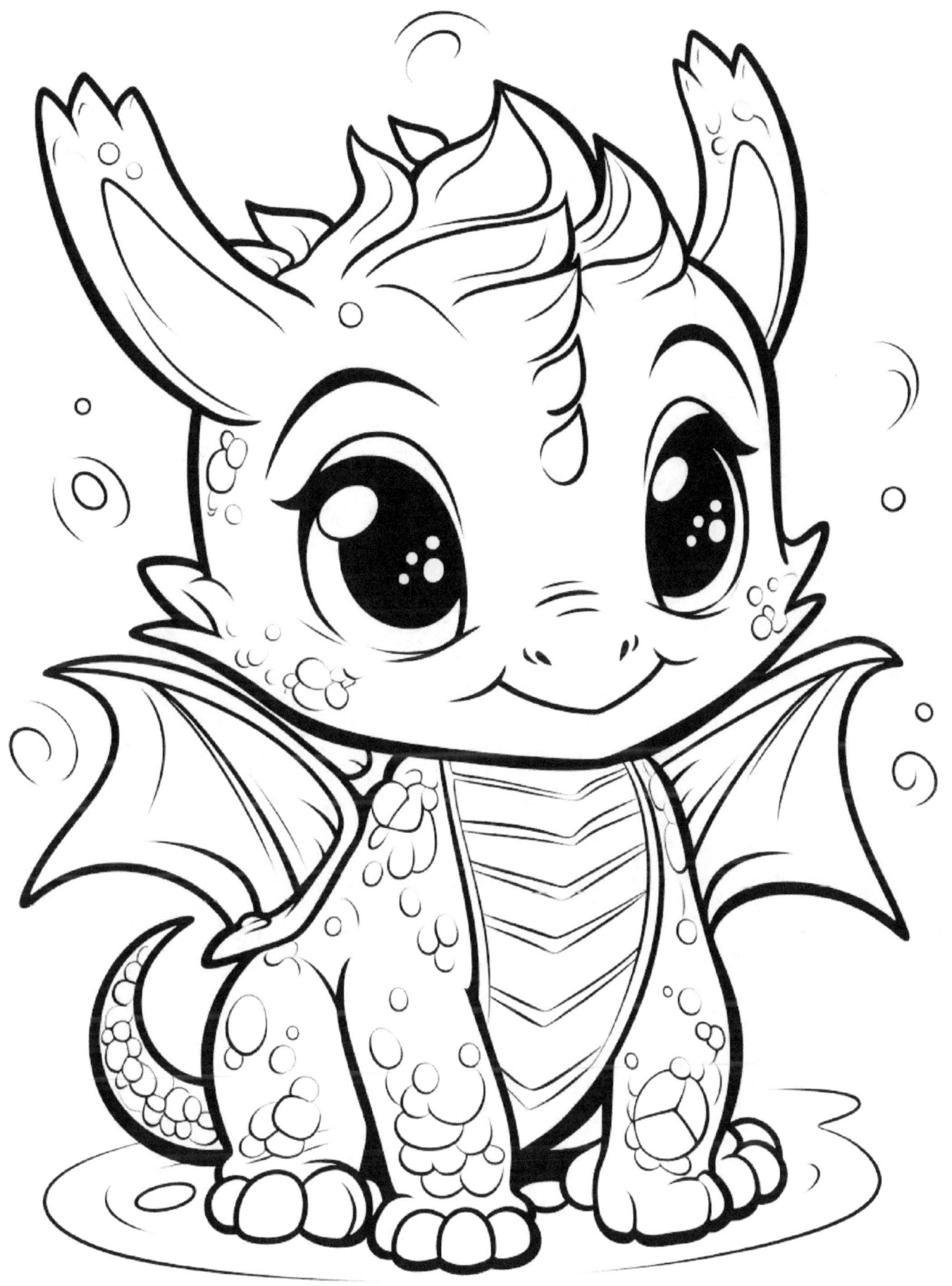

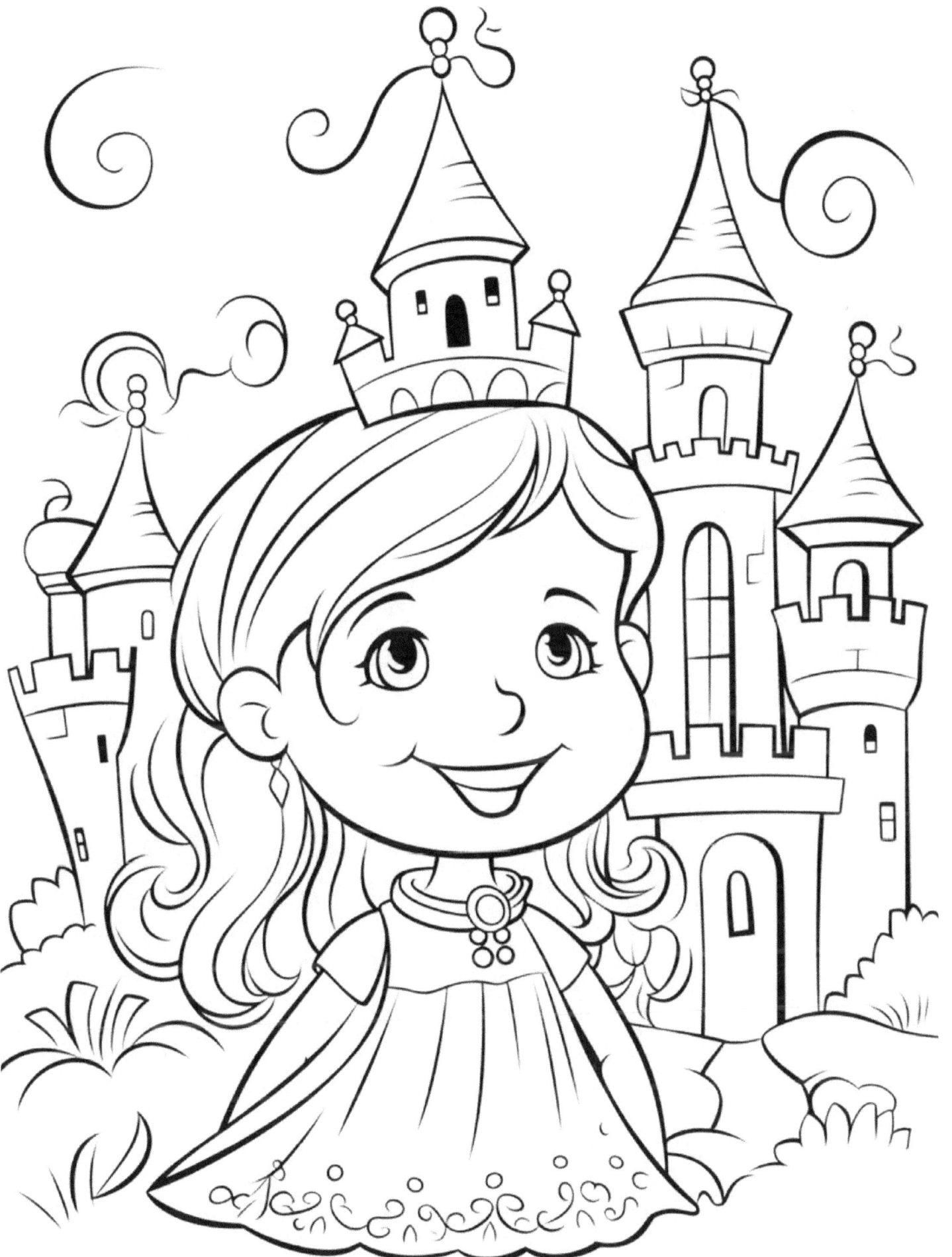

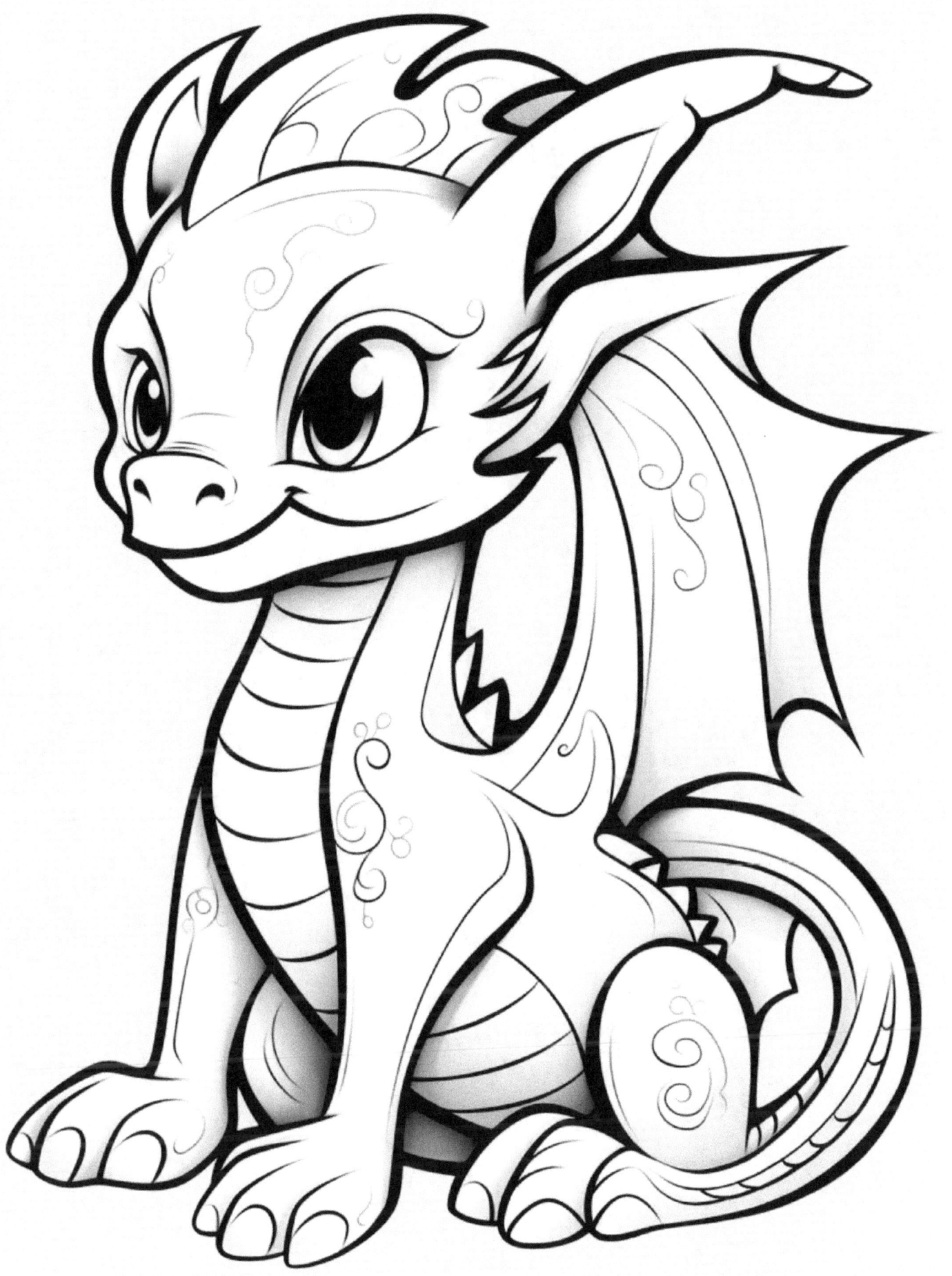

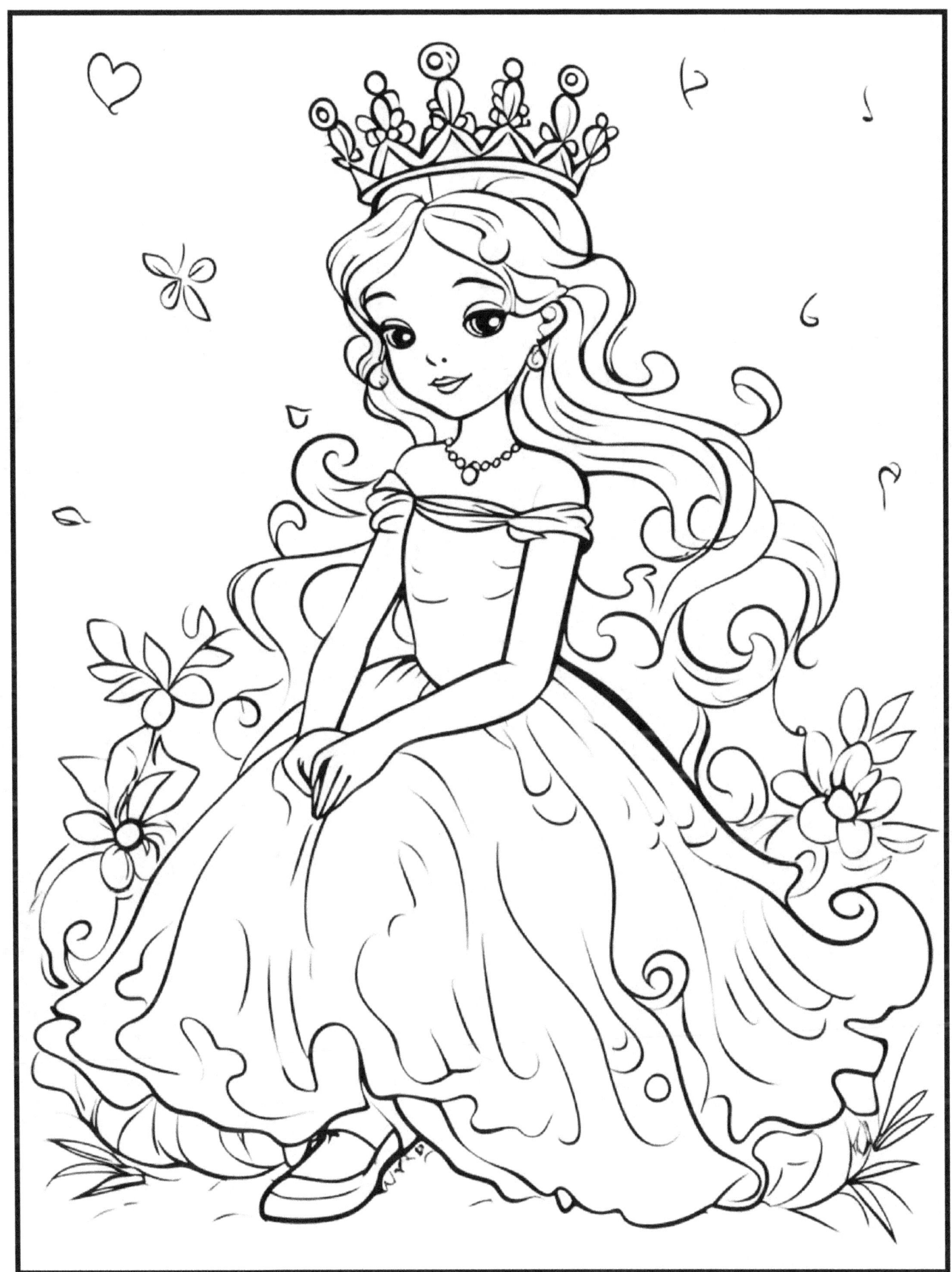

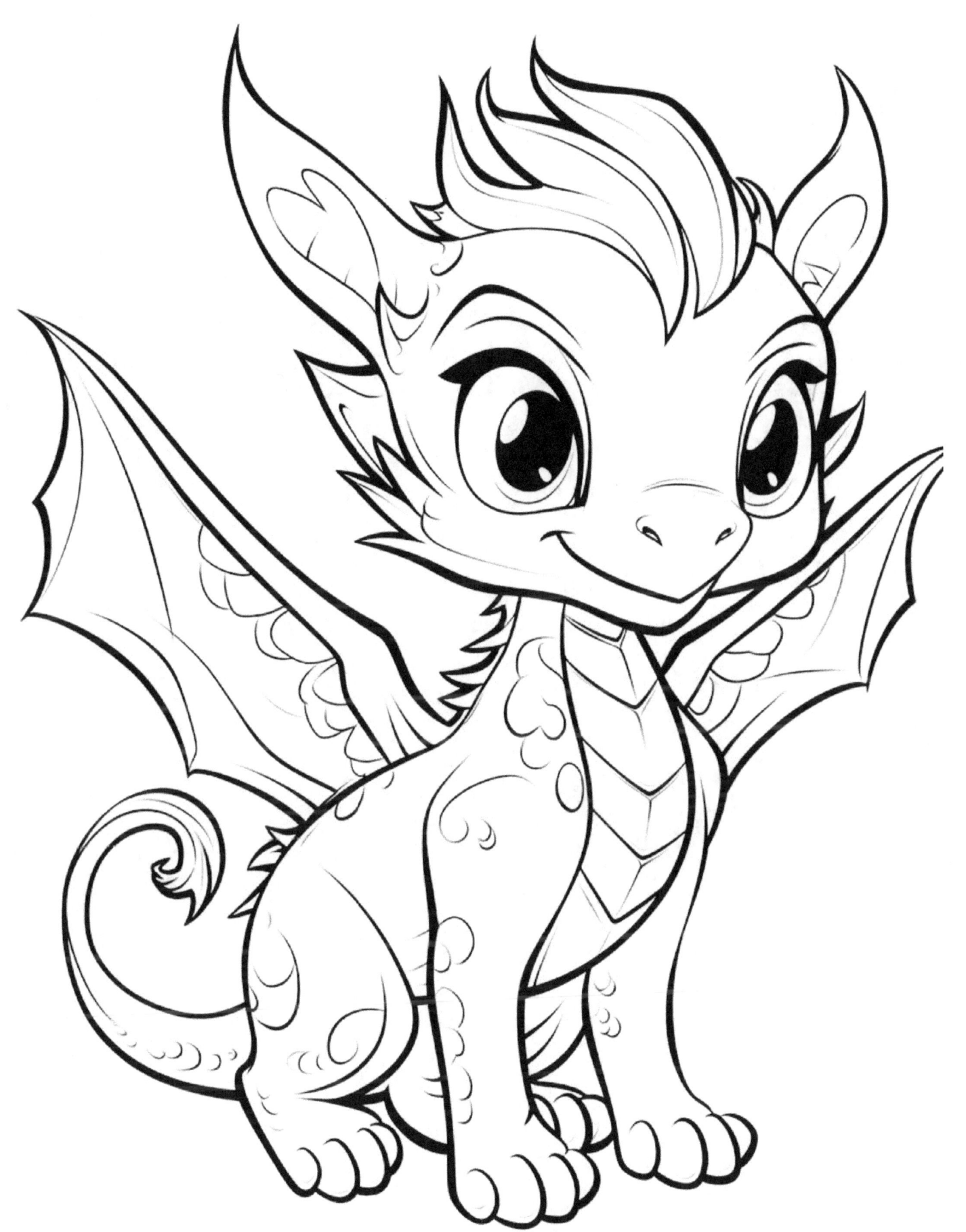

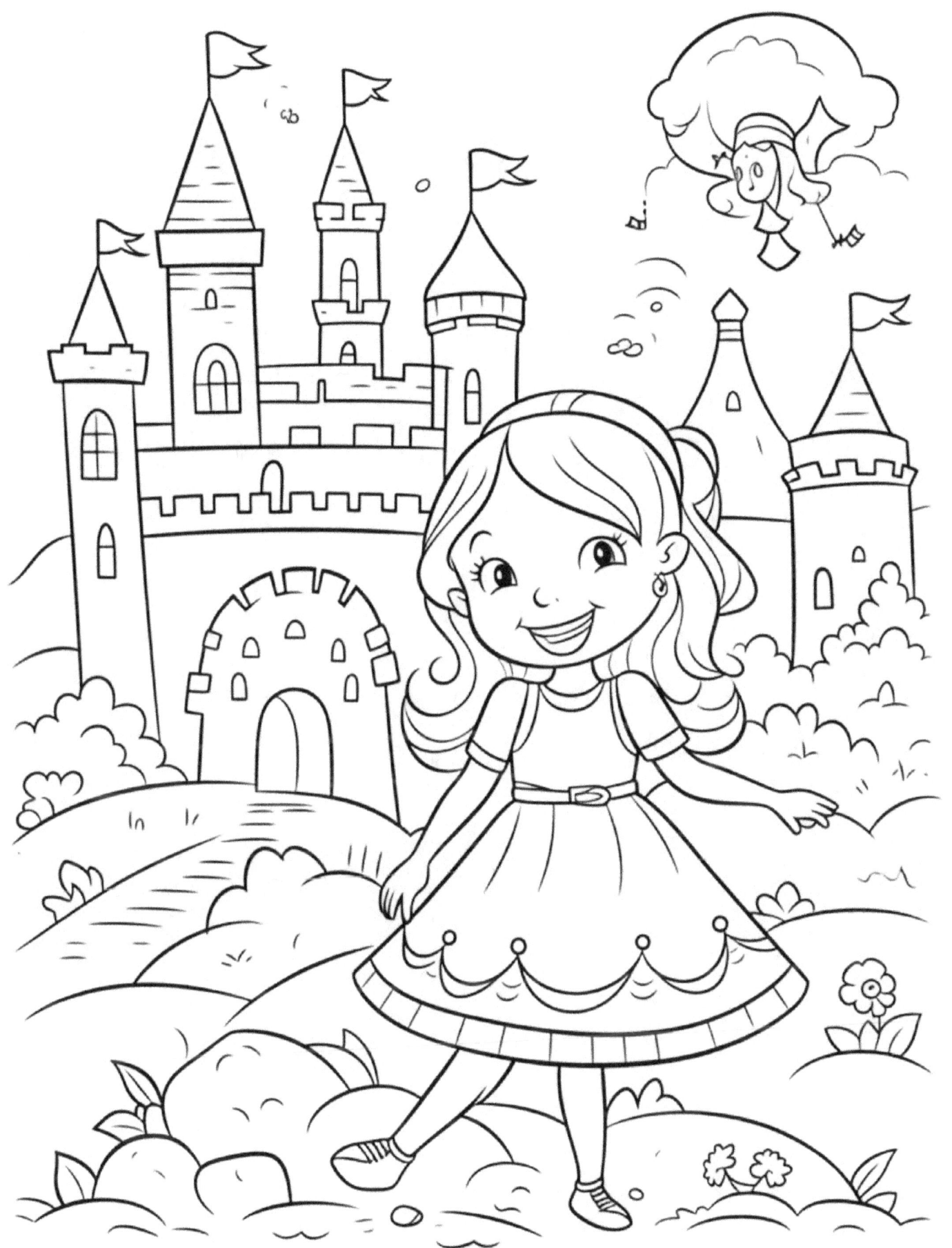

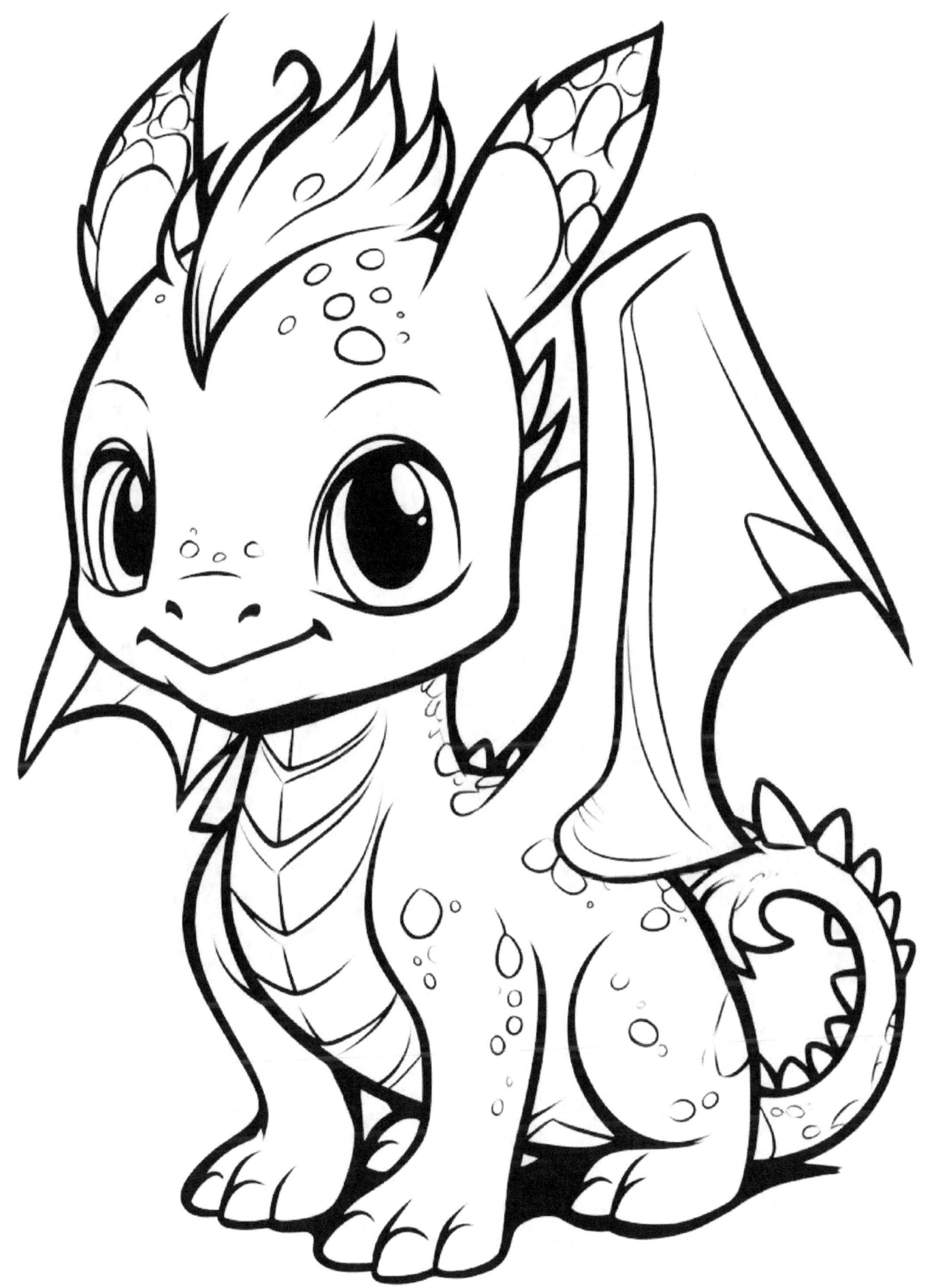

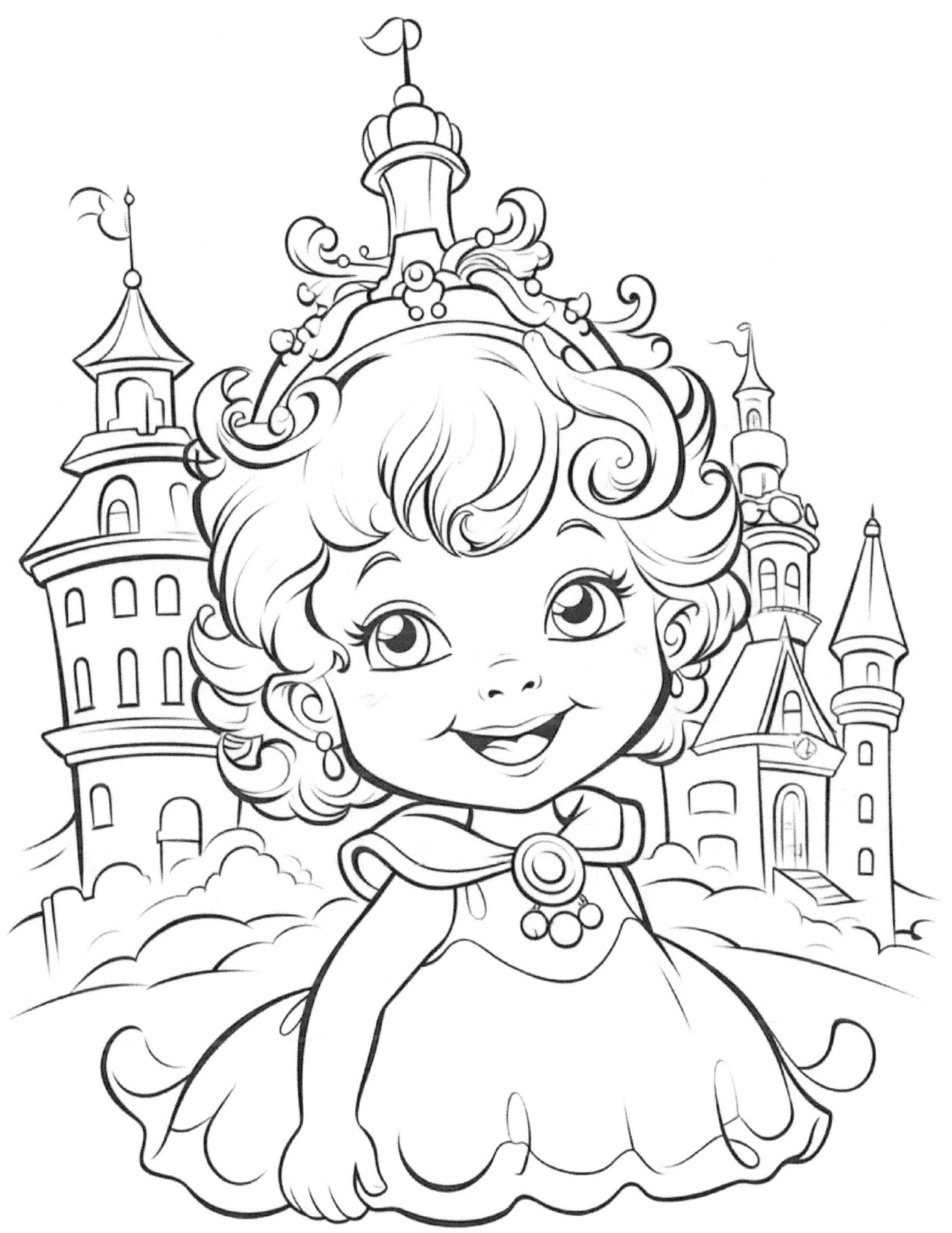

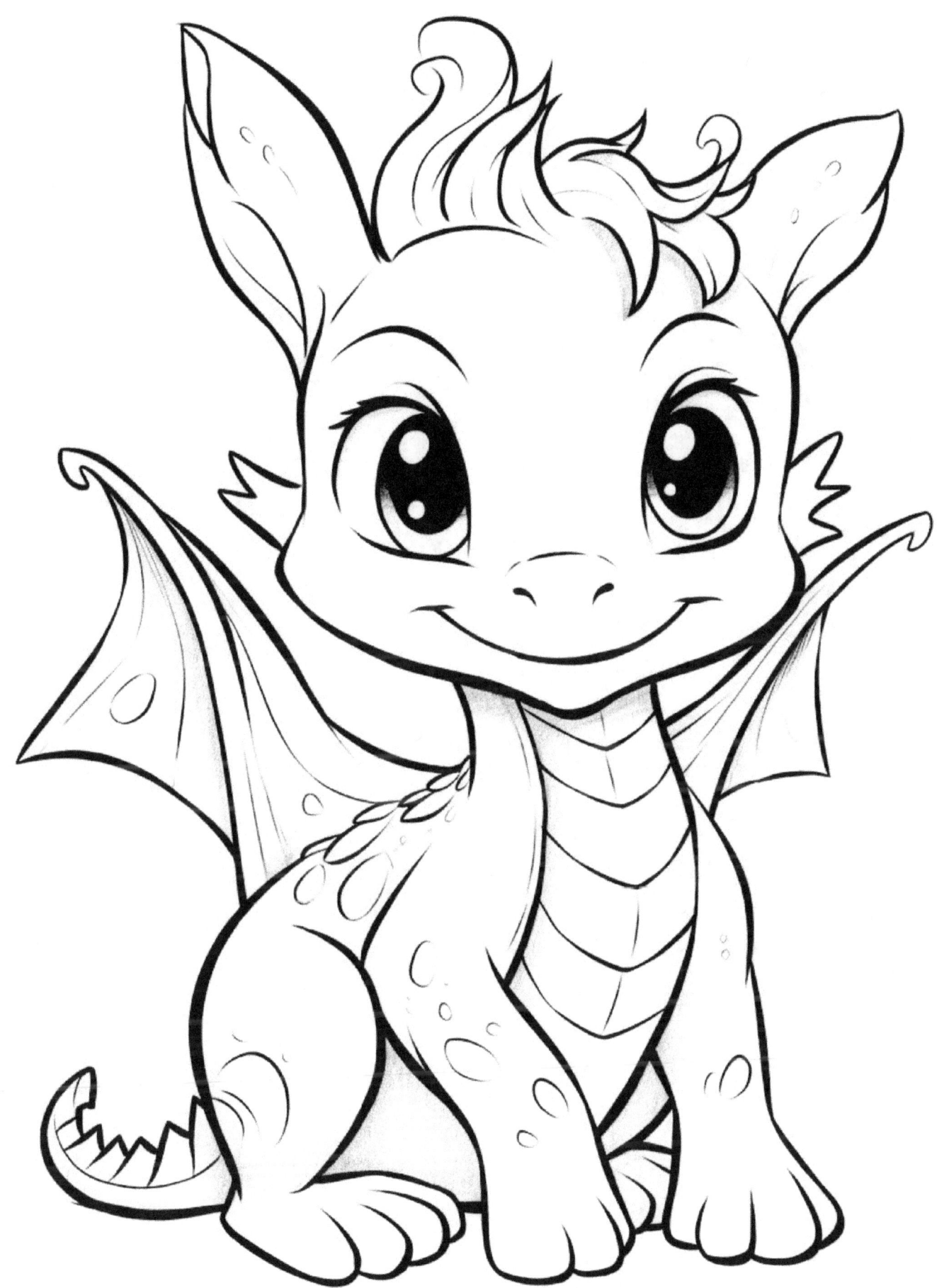

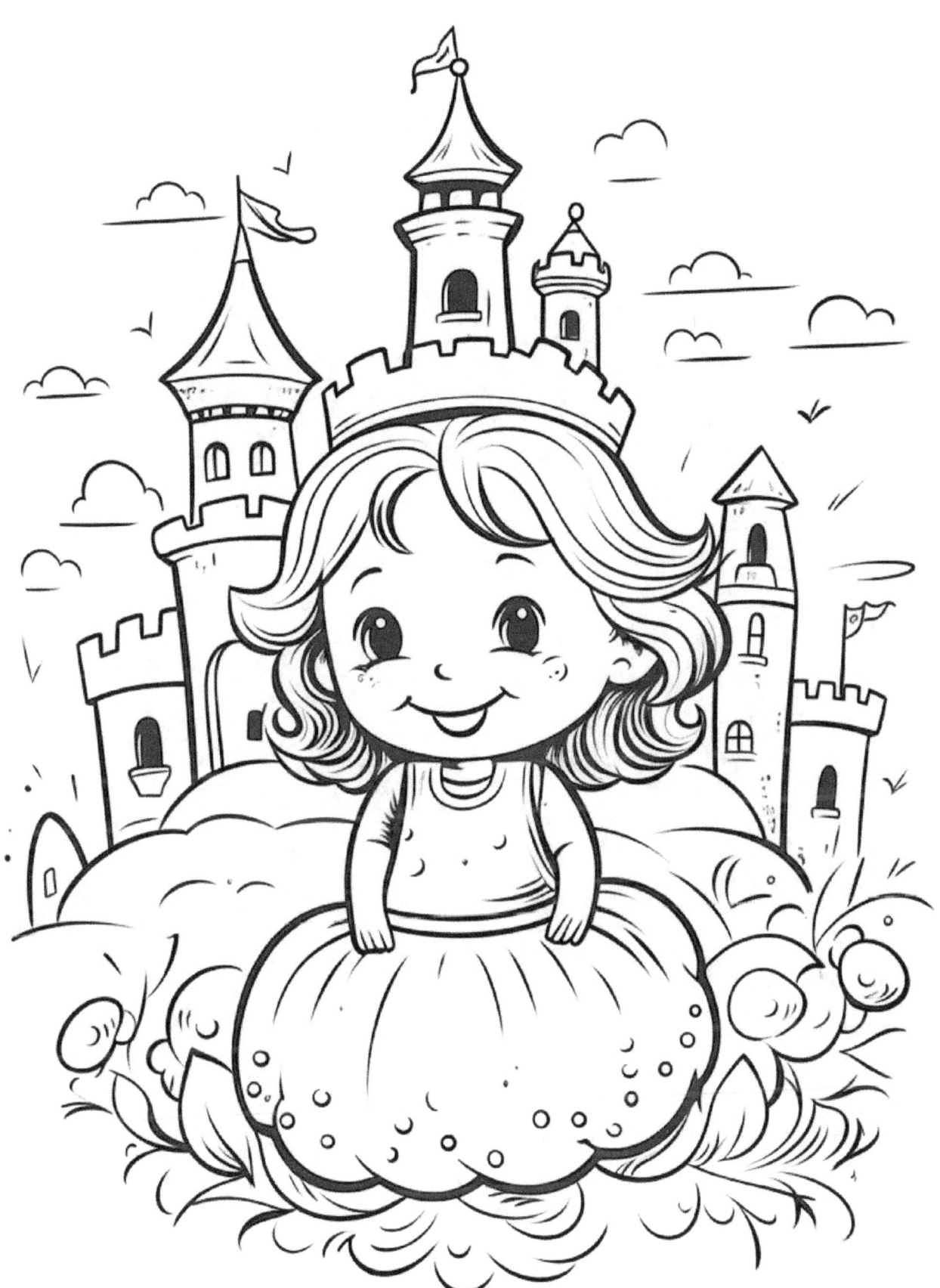

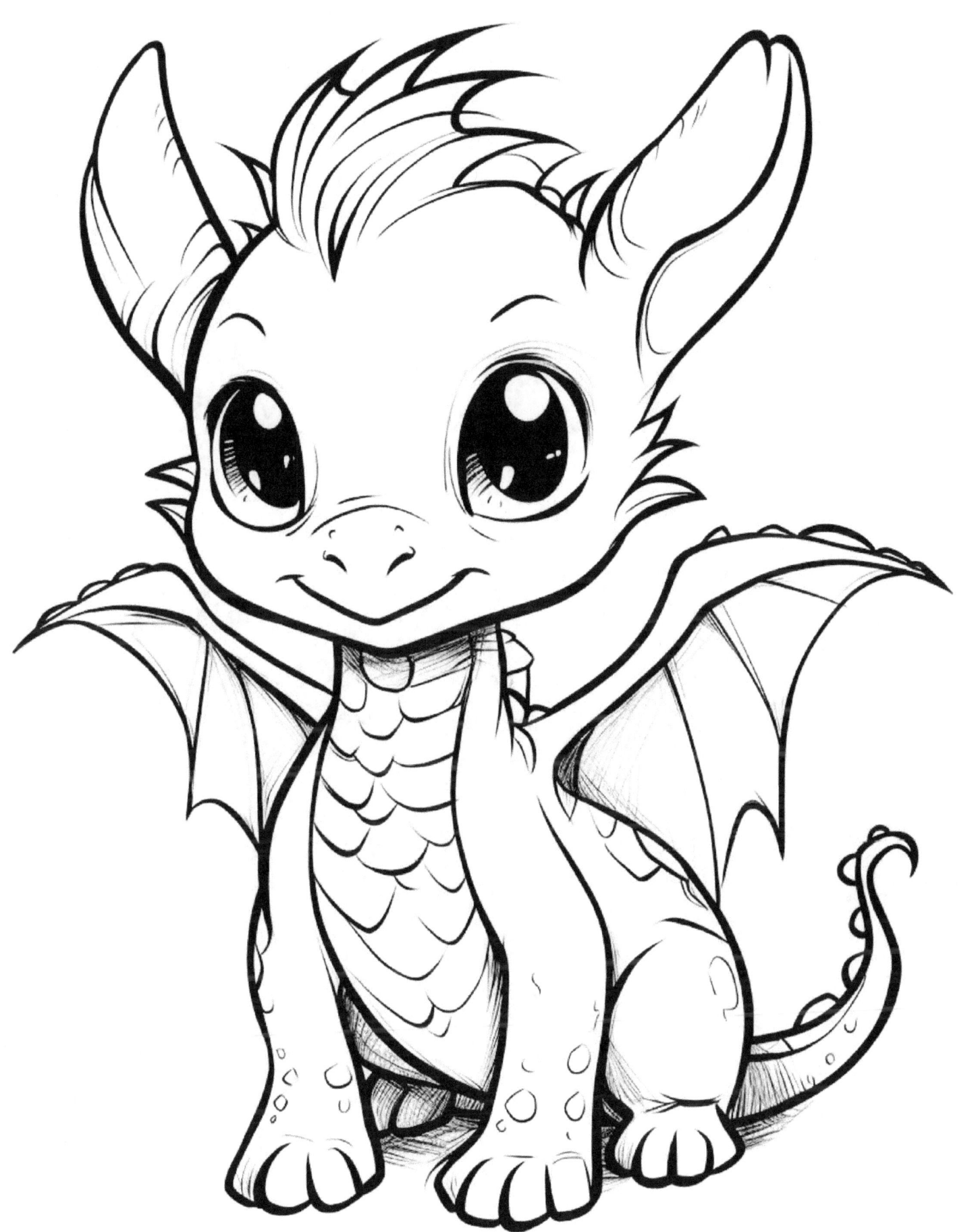

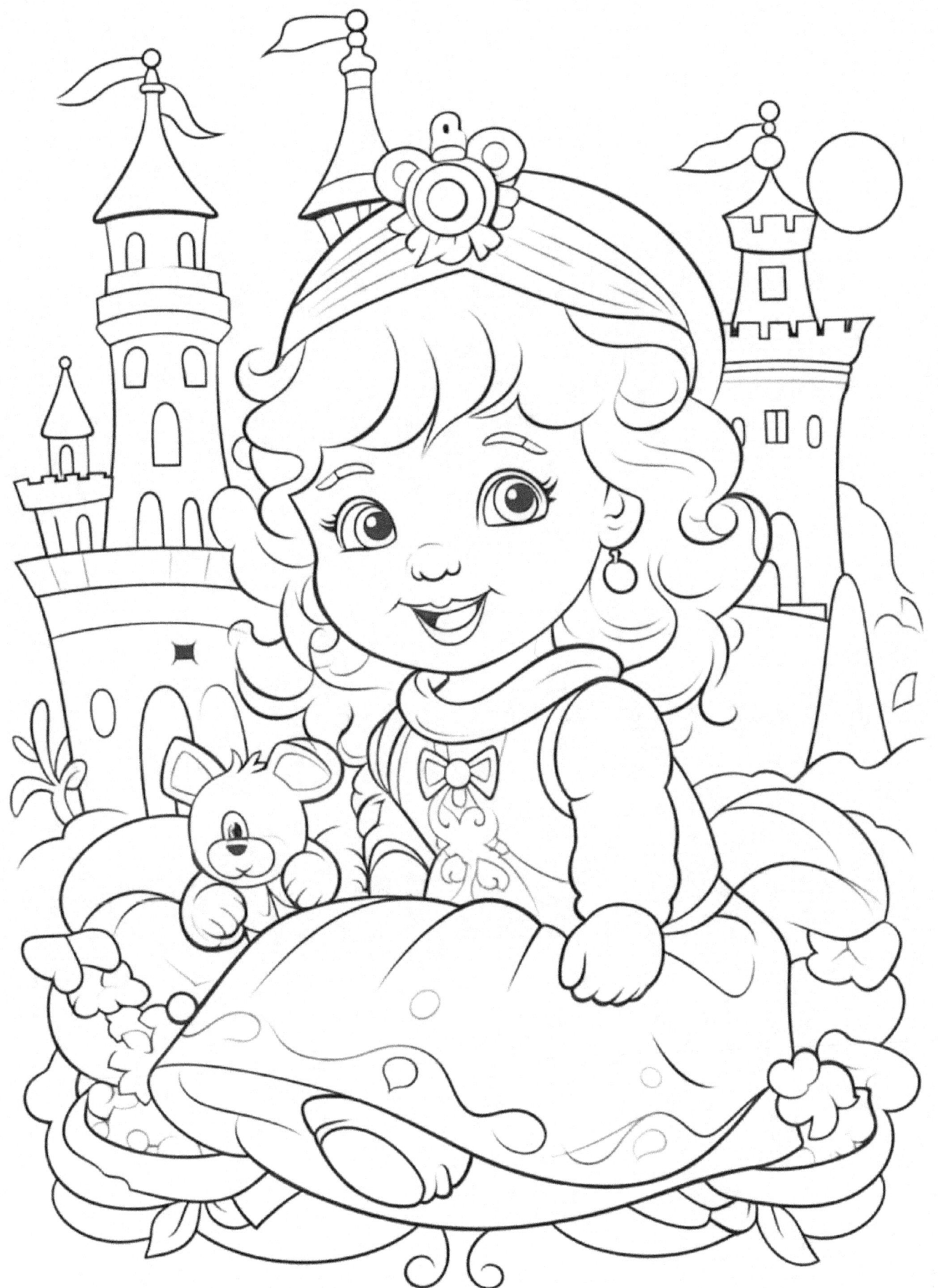

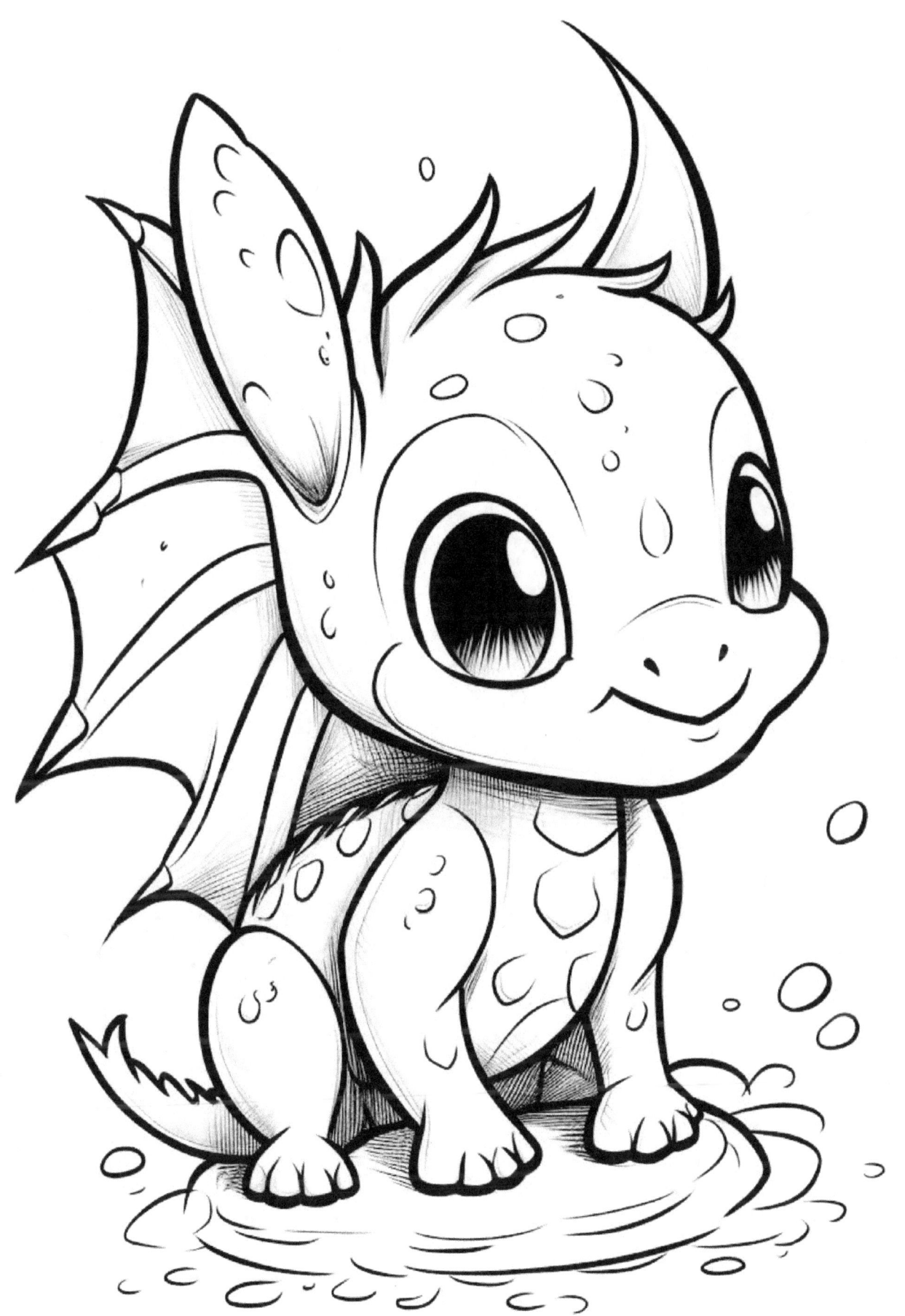

Thank You So Much For Spending Some Time Being Creative With Us.

Please take a look at some of our other activity and coloring books. As well as our large collection of journals.

AH64Designs

www.ingramcontent.com/pod-product-compliance
Lightning Source LLC
Chambersburg PA
CBHW082222220526
45470CB00010B/3281